More Essays on Everything

A Little More Sublime, A Little Less Ridiculous With Lots More In Between

MARGARET STORTZ

ISBN: 1497308550
ISBN 13: 9781497308558
Library of Congress Control Number: 2014905018
CreateSpace Independent Publishing Platform
North Charleston, South Carolina

To The Readers.....

For whose interest and pleasure I write...

Other Books by Margaret Stortz

Essays on Everything – From the Sublime to the Ridiculous with a little in between

Lights Along The Way – Concise Histories and Comparisons of Three American Metaphysical Belief Systems: Christian Science, Unity, and Religious Science

I am Enough – And Other Wisdom for Daily Living

Start Living Every Day of Your Life

Table of Contents

On New Beginnings

I would imagine that a new-born infant, gulping in its first breaths of air, is about the newest beginning there is, with glints of the Infinite flashing in its unfocused eyes. Doubtless the child is influenced somewhat by the inner and outer circumstances surrounding it, but mostly it is a *tabula rasa*, a clean slate awaiting new impressions. And impressions begin immediately. Is the child wanted, cared for? Is it a careless mistake? Is its surrounding one of love and support; or does it seem foreign and hostile? There are any number of things and situations that can either uplift or mar a new beginning.

Yes, it matters how a new beginning is set forth, but it is but one of an endless series. Author, Wilferd Petersen, who wrote the delightful *Art of Living* books during the early 20th Century, said that "every day is a lifetime in miniature." Regardless of what happened the day before, each day offers an opportunity to push a re-set button and begin all over again. This is an essential truth, and it can also be a fact, but only if we are willing to shake off the effects of the previous day, good or bad, and not haul the still-warm memories of the past into a waiting dawn. Some days become a post mortem; we can recall their events, see what worked and what didn't and move on, newly taught. The sailors involved in the latest America Cup Races did exactly that...held a daily post mortem. Each evening they examined each race and determined what they could do better the next day...but then that day was done, and the next race on the next day stood afresh before them.

Lots of us tend not to be so surgical in our handling of the events of the day. Sometimes there are no post mortems, just the accumulation of blame and guilt that occurs around our real or imagined failures...and it never shuts off. It sits just outside our eyelids, waiting for us to wake up and start all over again. There can't be new beginnings when our minds are so engaged. There can only be continuations of what was. The day, the opportunity, the event before us is already old and already marked.

Some people can get so weighed down by the string of yesterdays they drag along that they won't even cast an eager eye at a new sunrise. There is great sadness here and a genuine unawareness of all that we have been given. I think some of us just give up when we could make another choice. These days we really can do more into advancing age. I keep looking for the "magic bullet," the one that will erase a few wrinkles, but in the meantime, I'll be my own bullet and keep peeking around corners. I remember a famous statement made by New York Yankees ball player, Yogi Berra. He said, "It ain't over 'til it's over." You know, he's right...it ain't!

On Brailling

My husband and I got together in the middle of our lives, which meant that we brought into our relationship our already established opinions, attitudes and behaviors, formed long ago in our young lives. My, were we capable of heady conversations, and, shall we say, "spirited discussions!" Quiet exchanges actually did take place and were always possible, but often loud and noisy were more the norm, especially during our early years together.

Then we got smart. We both knew that, as controlling as we both were, we were not about to change one another, so we had to find a way to make it through verbal communications without committing mayhem, and we invented...brailling. Everyone knows about the splendid language called Braille, created by French teacher, Louis Braille, in the 19th Century, that enables the blind to read using a coded system of raised dots that they could touch with their fingers. Quite simply they "read" with their fingers, and if they wished, did not make a single sound. Well, as my husband and I discovered, there were lots of ways to be blind that did not necessarily involve physical sight. There were lots of ways to exhibit deafness as well that also did not involve physical hearing. We loved each other very much and were also quite blind and deaf at times to one another, not listening and not seeing what the other was trying to say.

So we taught each other to braille our bodies. We learned to recognize the point of no return in our heated discussions, the point where if anyone said one more word, one more syllable, one tiny snort...we were into it! Full-on hollering! No opportunity to say anything lest it stoke a verbal forest fire. Instead we reached out to use the language of touch. We might not have had the sense to say "I love you," but we could pass the words through our fingers, and we did. Quite often for awhile. The wonder of a soft touch on the arm or shoulder, a finger or two brushing the back of the neck...and the anger backed away, the fires blew out. We were wise enough not to intrude any sexual overtures in the touching, which would have lost us the chance to simply love as people growing in love again.

By now we've learned a couple of things. We don't engage in much silly stuff anymore, so the need for big-time brailling isn't there. Still, we both learned a whole, new language together. Belonging can be conveyed in so many ways; Oneness shows up when we least expect it sometimes. We have come to know each other so well that the exchange of a single touch can speak more volumes than the spoken word ever could.

Riding together in the car, no words exchanged yet the desire to speak love surfacing, it is so natural, so easy to touch a knee, rest a hand on the thigh, saying once more for the zillionth time...I love you.

On Doorknobs

One morning I woke up completely saturated with silliness and decided that I could write small essays on just about anything. Somehow I settled on doorknobs. This choice proved to be a goofier quest than I had imagined. Who in his right mind gives a damn about door knobs? Doorbells... maybe...at least they can be musical and sound as gongs or play little ditties for us. And then there are doorknockers which can become big deals in themselves. Who has not seen pictures at least of some grandiose doorknockers that hold a thunderous striker that can cause the entire door to tremble? Perhaps some estates welcome the visitor with a great lion's open jaws, holding a brass striker. This is impressive and artful, certainly indicative of a grander, bygone era.

But doorknobs! C'mon...they are already below the line of vision, unless you happen to be three years old, and mostly they are locked, to keep the outsider a perpetual outsider. How many doors have we come to where no one responded to our knock...even if people were inside...and so no doorknob turned to allow us entry. Doorknobs then acted as sentries, only turning when selected persons were allowed inside.

Doorknobs could be indicative of doors in the early days of this country that no longer exist. As a child growing up in San Francisco, our family lived at times in some of the old Victorians built in certain districts. One in particular stands out in memory because it had a beveled glass doorknob that seemed like a jewel to a little girl. If I grow quiet for a moment, the feel of that special doorknob with its rises and falls comes to my fingertips.

Perhaps I'm giving doorknobs a bad rap. When people are creating a very special home, built from the ground up or extensively remodeled, every detail becomes important, and we become aware that even the most seemingly mundane thing, like a doorknob, adds to the life of the whole. They become an item; they become unique. Just the right one is needed to invite visitors to feel welcome as they come to the door.

Now and again there are doors without knobs on them. Sometimes these are slide doors, shed doors or garden doors, and there is the scurry to find entry if we do not know where to look. Is there a latch somewhere off to one side? Does a spring hinge keep it closed? A door with only a keyhole before us would involve someone's key or someone on the other side of the door to open it for us. Somehow this seems a bit unnatural or out of joint. There really should be a doorknob for us to grasp as an obvious way in.

Interesting, isn't it, how something as inconsequential as a doorknob, one of the least things among us, can hold meaning we might never have considered. I wonder how many of these inconsequentials we routinely overlook.

On Compassion

To be fully human I believe we have to learn and practice compassion. We are not born with this very human quality. We have to come to it through desire and a certain amount of civilizing because it is the effort to become a civilized person that makes us aware of others. We have to outgrow the cave man mentality and come together as caring humans, part of a group that thinks of the good of the whole as well as each individual member.

The nature of compassion is such that it causes us to think of the needs of others as well as our own. The idea of this is very simple, certainly not rocket science, but the practice of it takes the best of us to make the extension to another when his needs are clear. It is also clear that we may have to forbear when something we might do could harm another. I believe that when we behave in these ways, it is our spirituality that is in action. Perhaps we could even consider the compassionate "us" as God-like, even if we have to work at it. And why not, for love and compassion certainly go hand in hand, and I'm not sure we can have the one without the other.

There is no pain in being compassionate. We are not asking others to do what we want them to do. The person who assists someone who is disabled is not asking that person to become whole again, at least not physically. Rather, the love that accompanies the compassionate worker is part of the expertise that a care giver brings. It is part of the giving without asking for something in return. There may, of course, be a return, through smiles and gratitude on the part of the receiver, but the compassionate act is the choice of the one who assists. So many have said that doing for others brings a great sense of well being. I think there is something mystical in this because others watching a compassionate act being done are themselves affected. I have asked myself: What is taking place? What has been engaged or set off? As a believer I think it has to be shared Oneness energized, pulling in everyone in its orbit.

The great spiritual leader, His Holiness, the Dalai Lama, has long been recognized as a champion of compassionate living, and to this he has dedicated his whole life, so much so that he has said that "love and compassion are necessities, not luxuries. Without them humanity cannot survive." Stellar thoughts, but often relegated to the "soft" side of life, good aims if we did not have to maintain the warrior cultures we have long established. If we did not have to protect ourselves from warring "others," perhaps we could open to love and com-passion. On the other hand, what might happen if we opened instead with loving concern for the other? Could it be possible we might change the world?

On Dusting Off Home Plate

Baseball is the only game I really know. Oh, I know what basketball and football intend with their baskets and goal posts, and I understand what the goalie's job is in soccer, but these sports are way too fast for me. Too much racing back and forth on courts and up and down on fields. When I was a kid there was nothing better than sitting in the ballpark in the warm sun watching a pitcher wind up and let loose a 90-mile-an-hour fast ball. And when the game was a little slow, as it often was, you could nip out for a beer (or in my case, a coke) and a hotdog. I understood the calls. I knew what a line drive was, a looping fly ball, or a Texas leaguer. Indeed, these were great, growing up years.

What memory brings up for me now is something the umpire did many times during a game. When home plate got covered over by too much dust and dirt, so much so that it was hard to find its parameters, the umpire would stop the entire course of the game, pull out a dinky little whiskbroom and dust off home plate. Then, of course, things started up again. Over the years I remembered the clever action, but didn't think a lot about it. In my sports nostalgia, I think about it now because that small act seems so symbolic of the ways in which the rational mind can work.

As I think back, it now makes perfect sense why home plate had to be kept clear. If a pitcher's throw was close, it could be very hard to call a ball or strike if the base was not clearly visible. Only the umpire's eye could be trusted, and he needed the best view he could get. Naturally he protected his view. Recently I have been wondering if this sweet little metaphor could not find its way into our busy lives today.

We may not be out in the field throwing pitches or catching flies, but we're doing a lot of dodging and weaving in the course of the day. Now that we have so much technology at our fingertips, we don't have to move so thoughtfully through what is at hand. Spell check doesn't catch everything, though, so we still have to proof our own work, and as much as I love the ease of using a computer, sometimes I fear that I am developing its mentality. I want programs and answers to appear in seconds, no searching, no pauses, no hesitations, minimum effort on my part.

Good thing I still have a little of the quiet, thinking mind in me. I can stop the harried actions, the mistakes made due to haste. I can remember the meaning of the umpire's decision to stop the game's action for a few moments, and I can take time to dust off home plate and be clear again...naturally.

On WWII

I remember WWII, only in small ways perhaps since I was a little child during its span of time. But I remember it. Because our family lived on the west coast, I remember the black-out curtains we had to pull down whenever the shrill, air raid siren blared. I remember watching its progress on the Movietone News during Saturday matinees, only it was always a week or so late. No on-the-spot reporting then. I knew that families suffered awful losses of brothers or fathers who didn't come back, but ours did not suffer this. My uncle had a ship shot out from under him, but I didn't know this until years later. You didn't tell little kids about those near misses if you didn't have to.

My awareness of the Great War, or so it was called, did not expand until years later when I learned that a family friend was part of the Bataan death march. It lived in his eyes, but he never spoke of it. I learned from an African-American friend what it was like to be a black man in a segregated military.

And somewhere, for some reason, among those of a certain generation, World War Two simply became identified as WWII, as if it were a chunk of history rewarded with its own special acronym.

This was the war in which more Americans were killed than in any other military conflict, with the exception of the American Civil War where we killed ourselves. This was not the case in other countries where Jews and Russians died in the millions, and not always in direct military action. In its vastness and destruction, this war was so terrible that it was supposed to end all wars. Now, as we think of small wars, conflicts, incursions, invasions…as we think of years of détente, brinksmanship and missile rattling, we can almost smile at the naïveté of a young nation quickly growing older over broken promises, constant threats, and the extortions of manufactured crises

Since the Great War, can any of us remember a time when war or the threat of war was not out there on the horizon somewhere? Can we even imagine a consciousness of peace spreading over the world, even in our wildest hopes and dreams? You would think so. You would think that the urge to live without armed conflict when so many have lost so much would overwhelm mass awareness to the point where all would refuse to even look at a weapon. Not so. Not while we still fear and loath that which is different. Not while we covet what our neighbor has, and not while we still invest in studying war and not peace. Is there light? Is there hope? Of course. No mother raises up a child only to see it killed. Reprising the thoughts of Israeli Prime Minister, Golda Meir, we could say that when we love our children more than we hate the other, there will be peace.

On Being a Citizen

Recently on the front page of the newspaper, I saw a picture of a naturalization ceremony that took place in a nearby major city. The camera in its cleverness focused clearly on an alert young man who was listening intently to the proceedings, while it gave a soft focus to everyone around him. The look on his face was almost beatific, and as he held a small American flag close to his body, he seemed immersed in his own light. Camera tricks perhaps, but the young man appeared to b a worthy representative of the newly-minted Americans. A former Nepalese mountain guide, the man spoke of being very proud of his achievement and, as so many new citizens said in one way or another, he uttered that "everything in the U.S. is great..."

The young, former Sherpa reminded me of another man who clamored to become a U.S. citizen many decades ago. Making his way across Eastern Europe, so torn to pieces by

WW II, he eventually made his way to America and later into my heart as my husband. Like the Sherpa, he thought America was the best country in the world, and after all these years and all that he knows of his adopted country's shortcomings, he still does. He is my favorite patriot.

When I think of my husband, having lived the bulk of his life on American shores, and the young Nepalese man, whose citizenship documents contain ink that is barely dry, I wonder: What do they know about this country that we American born have forgotten or never did know? Is it like the Catholic convert who knows more about the sacred ceremonies of his chosen religion than those baptized as infants? Are the fruits of freedom and possibility so scattered on the ground around us that we no longer see them?

I'm not a jingoist, and I don't believe the hype about America's specialness, but I do know a good thing when I see it. I suspect I know this because of the cast that comes to my husband's eyes whenever he thinks of his coming to America... to find me, he says slyly. But before me there was his desire to make a new home, and he did. What I believe the old patriot and the young one share is a sense of citizenship that most native born never think about. We do not know of hard-won entry into this land, entry so desired by some that they throng across our borders, sometimes legally, sometimes not. Many of us have become infected by something called consumerism, and we are referred to by both government and corporations as consumers, not citizens. Many have forgotten that a free people have to value and protect the very freedoms they have simply taken for granted.

Causes for thought, I think, and maybe some action, such as making sure no election cycle passes without our vote or government act goes unnoticed. What would it be like to feel like a citizen, perhaps for the very first time, even if we have lived our entire lives in this land?

On Random Acts of Kindness

After 9/11 we Americans learned that our assump-
tions of general safety were not as unassailable as we
thought. In fact we have become more aware of our vulnerabili-
ties to armed attack, even as we go about our business as ordinary citizens. It seems we have not only nature's rampages
to contend with---hurricanes, earthquakes, fires and floods-
--now we have nameless, faceless enemies looking for "soft"
targets to destroy. I believe in these years we have grown aware
of an ambiguous overtone of dismay that overlays us as a
populace. It is difficult to view ourselves as a united citizenry
right now. Instead we seem to be sorted out into irritable tribes
gathering into pockets of alienation, satisfied only when we
are with our own. People who would normally be interesting to
us now just look like strangers and are not to be trusted.

After one particularly odious bomb attack, I suddenly
became awake to something that always happens after such

disasters, and I mean always. Almost in an instant, once the smoke begins to clear, people "come to," so to speak, and begin to help. Certainly there are rescue workers trained in disaster work and they arrive as soon as possible, but I am thinking of ordinary people who turn to do whatever is at hand. The ubiquitous media coverage and social networking began at once to stream pictures of people carrying injured folks out of harm's way. They may themselves have had bloodied faces, but they are aiding others. This particular bombing not only killed but also caused great injuries to limbs, causing necessary amputations. In all the reporting coming in, there was a call from a man that was nowhere on the scene who was himself am amputee. He reportedly said, "Call me when I can help people learn to live full lives again, even with missing arms or legs." Somewhere in all this disarray, someone coined the notion of engaging in "random acts of kindness," which is exactly what so many were busy doing as a natural response.

What is it that happens at these times? Is there some chemical, altruistic wiring in us that is activated during disasters? We can be snarling at each other over disputes and complaints one minute, and then jump into action during an emergency the next. I am not satisfied with the idea that some communal, preservative instinct is taking over. I am a believer. I believe that all life is joined in an eternal movement that we all share. Often we blow this off during the course of normal days. But let something out of the ordinary happen that jolts us out of our common lethargy, and the heart-to-heart connection becomes hyper activated. Massive love is mobilized; intense caring is heightened, and we do extraordinary things…going toward destruction to find and serve. Absolutely we are more than we think we are, and maybe we can find a better means of discovery, perhaps in acts of kindness that are intentional, not simply random.

On Smiling

For several years my husband and I walked the paths of a neighborhood park most week days; for exercise, yes, but also for a wonderful chance to be in an open space. During these years an older, Japanese man was walking also, only he walked in the opposite direction from us and would regularly cross our paths. He ambled along just about as slowly as my husband did, so our crossings came up in a measured way. I could easily see his grim face, a stern, closed visage. He never smiled, and we did not speak.

I am a great believer in the effectiveness of non-verbal communication, and I know of the invitation that smiling brings. Some think that we smile to keep people at bay, as if to say, "I'm harmless." I don't think so. I think that a smile, genuinely given, is an extension of ourselves to another, a gift of silent greeting. So I decided to smile this man into submission. Every time we would pass one another, I would smile a big, wide, kickass smile and accompany it with one of my favorite, silent greetings...I love you. Time after time I would do my little routine, and time after time he would simply pass me, stone-faced.

One day something different happened. The man smiled...not a big, toothy grin but a small pursing of lips with the corners turned up. And this continued, with the eventual uncovering of a few teeth showing. Over a period of months that eventually passed into years, those breaking smiles grew into short commentaries, exclamations about the weather, questions about our mutual health. Before our spate of time together finished, my Japanese friend and I became aware of each other's families, how many children we each had, when he would visit his daughters in Hawaii and such other things that people who grow to care about each other exchange. Over time both my friend and my husband became unable to walk the park's trails much and so only occasionally would we spot one another. At these times while my husband was seated, I would hurry over to him to catch up on our shared stories until eventually our contact slipped away.

These days as I think about the park times, I am amazed at how such a small gesture grew into a relationship with a life and history of its own. I wonder whether or not my friend still walks the earth...he was elderly when I first saw him....I wonder if he is enjoying the warm Hawaiian sun. I wonder if I were walking the park's paths again, would I make the same invitation once more to another solemn walker?

I think these are the questions that beset us all. In a world where technologies connect us through gadgets, we can find it easier to become isolated physically from others. It takes time and effort to craft a breathing relationship, and I fear time becomes contracted through the lack of need for personal connection. If another unsmiling person walked my way again, would I crack the first smile? I hope so.

On Shades of Gray

American politics are not very pretty these days. Actually they haven't been for some decades, but they seem somehow to be more unwary and uncivil than ever. I am not so naive' as to think that legislators will sit down and come up with agreed-upon, bipartisan solutions that will be universally acceptable. I know about the meaning of the "loyal opposition" and the purpose it serves. I also know that something in the governing process is very much out of whack and growing more so. Once legislators understood the meaning of the word, compromise. Now they seem to forbid its entry in simple conversation.

The wonderful concept of checks and balances, so valued in the American system, appears to have been set aside and replaced by unmovable ideologies. Congressional colleagues are not sitting down to talk; they are setting up oppositional camps. Flexible congressmen who may follow a general ideology are now being forced to become *ideologues*... guardians of "rightness", destroyers of "wrongness," without any concepts of shades of gray.

Those of us who do not have the power to force others to our will...or maybe have lost it as powerless relatives or companions have flown the coop...have come to understand the meaning of shades of gray. There are very few arenas of black vs. white and very few instances of incorruptible moralities. We sometimes cannot even sort out a viable good that will be recognized by all. We may settle on values and behaviors regarding our own persons that allow for no transgressions by anyone, but we cannot do this for another. So...we get shades of gray, not fully satisfactory, not fully unsatisfactory; not an entire loaf but some slices. Frankly, I think that people grow up when they have to wrestle with good ideas that are tipped with dark overtones. When we sweep away the ideologue's gavel, we can get down to the difficult, gritty thinking that allows us see that there are other points of view worthy of consideration.

Compromise is no fun... no fun at all. By its nature it means that no one gets all he or she wants. It contains irritation and unsettling, untracked pathways, but it is fraught with life. We could ask ourselves: Do I want to stick with a perceived idea of truth that may be deadly to some, or am I willing to consider that truth has many faces? Shades of gray do not mean vague, colorless concepts or ways of doing things that are not vital. Shades of gray move from dark to light, in to out, no to yes with lots of maybes along the way. If somehow we have built a seemingly insurmountable barrier between ourselves and the next man, shades of gray provide hammers and shovels for making holes in walls.

On Pain

I think I can safely say that there is no one among us who has not experienced pain. I say this because there are many kinds of pain, and not all of them are physical. When we think about it, we know that, at the very least, pain involves a disruption in the natural order of things. Any disruption causes discomfort, and this can go all the way from raging hurt in the body to great agitation in the mind when something does not proceed as we would wish.

Let's sort out a few ideas here. I believe that we as thinking beings are inheritors of a natural order of well being. If we are believers, we accept it as one of the gifts of the Spirit. If we are not, we can see ourselves as a part of nature in action. At any rate when the natural order is disturbed, we experience pain. Anyone who has had a physical operation knows that it is a process to remove disturbances and let the body's systems have their way again. The elimination of pain brings a return of comfort. Anyone who has borne a child knows that there is pain in the course of birth, but there is the wonderful pay-off of a new baby. People who are in chronic, physical pain, where there is not total elimination on hand, learn to manage it. This takes strength and courage and the determination that their lives will be under their control as much as possible, not waylaid by pain.

The pain that begins in the mind can be far more insidious. Enough mental pain will eventually affect the body, but before that happens, the raging discomfort in the mind will have unsettled the one who suffers terribly. Some are deeply troubled by unhealthy upbringings, failed relationships, lost opportunities, and experiences of loss...none of which can be changed. They can only surface in the mind. Memories of the past seem to intrude on the present so that the day is often overlaid by painful thoughts. I have found that these memories and the stories that form around them become very seductive. In a way they become almost like lovers, pulling us away from the things at hand, and they will take us hostage if we let them so that we are prisoners of our own thoughts.

Let us imagine for a while that the future has no pain. Yesterday's memories may contain some and sometimes the formations taking place today do, but the future is still ours to shape. Those in chronic, physical pain know the practices before them and have honed their skills. Those in mental pain actually have the best chance of healing because they can choose how they will think and what they will think. Today can be current and full of possibilities. The past does not have to be invited in. Our minds belong to us, and we are the ones who determine whether we live in mental freedom or bondage.

On Possibilities

Yay, possibilities! Where would we be without them? Stuck in the way it's always been...that's where. Still, on further thought, I think we'll find that this comment is not actually correct. We may not be noticing but things and situations do not stay the same; they are changing right along, and if we are not participating, they will change right out from under us. Children grow up, with or without our attention and guidance. Relationships, like fires, will go out if they are not stoked and tended.

Subtle changes are always in the works until they become big changes and finally get our attention, which causes me to ask: What are we missing? Are we oblivious to what is ours to do? I believe that we have the raw material in us to live fulfilled lives, but this is never done by accident. There needs to be attention and intention in us to become more of who we really are, and it is possibility that opens that door.

The trouble with it is that it involves the unknown, which is also the best of possibility as well. If we knew how efforts would turn out, this would not be a possibility. This would be a known target before us. But the unknown? That's frightening, and to approach it involves an element of risk taking. This does not necessarily mean leaping out of an airplane to try sky diving unless the jumper likes an adrenaline rush, but it can mean poking into an unexplored idea to see what it has for us.

I think that new ideas are just as fearsome as trying physical adventures. I also think that, if we are paying attention, we will find that sitting on our tush too long breeds irritation and sometimes sickness, maybe of the heart, maybe of the body. Author, Anais Nin, coined a wonderful phrase: "...And the day came when the right to remain tight in a bud was more painful than the risk it took to blossom." All infants of any kind know this intuitively. They are, after all, beings in the bud, and they simply must begin to blossom. Will the infant child refuse to learn to walk? Will the baby bird not spread its wings?

I think it is our perceived failures over time that close off possibility thinking...perhaps too many buds unopened or too many misfired blossomings. Nevertheless Nin's artful construct remains before us. We can take failure to mean many things. It can be a reason to try again, or it can be a reason never to venture forth and have another go. In the simplest way of all we could see that every dawning day holds possibility in it. There may be ordinary expectations embedded in it, but there is also the promising sunrise that has not yet made it to sunset. There is the piece of the day that we cannot control, an unknown unfolding that we cannot anticipate. Within these folds lies possibility, maybe unbidden, even unwanted, but here lies the bud.

On Spirituality

I believe that everyone is spiritual, actually everything, for that matter. I think that spirituality is the infinite essence that underlies all of life and eventually makes its way into form as well. We tend to think of spirituality as being an invisible movement, something that remains only in the mind in the realm of ideas, but I think that it also inhabits the shapes and forms of our lives and is consistently taking form and leaving form, very much like what death does for a body that is not longer useful. In a way, death acts as a cleansing agent; it does not obliterate life; it only removes an impediment to it. All the while our spirituality remains intact and as far as we know, continues to move as an essence until and unless it takes another form for greater ease of expression. This makes perfect sense to me, but then, I am a believer.

Over the eons of time, spirituality and religion have become mixed up together, with religion claiming a corner on the spirituality market. This has not always been a happy partnership, for organized religion has often completely missed the flowing freedom that characterizes the nature of spirituality and tried to cram it into rigid demands and codes. Is there really a right way to be spiritual...and a wrong way? Is it possible to be unspiritual, or are we just not adhering to a religious system's idea of correctness? More importantly, can the fulfillment of our spiritual natures be denied us by anything other than our own lack of understanding? Who can possibly know for us what we can only know for ourselves? Good questions that need to be asked, even if we are not sure about the answers.

As the centuries passed we got better and better at being religious. We gave our spirituality names and made it into gods that behaved like us. Sometimes Love sneaked into the mix, but a whole lot of time we were dealing with gods that were really mean spirited, wrathful and vengeful. As a young person I gave up on religion as such. I figured I already knew how to be miserable. Who needed a god that was better at it then I was? But spirituality, on the other hand...that never left, and its beckonings were never far off. It was, after all, essential to my nature. I didn't have to "get" it; I only had to become aware. Awakening after a night's sleep does not mean we have to create the daylight. We only have to step into it.

The genii is out of the bottle, as far as I am concerned. I cannot go back to the rightness and wrongness of organized religion. As the Sufi poet, Rumi, suggests I can only move past those highly structured ideas and meet others in the field of spirituality we all share. Imagine what it might be like if we all did.

On Imagination

When we think of using imagination, we often have before us the picture of crackling energies going out into the world, changing everything in its path. No doubt that this happens often; imagination changes things. What do think tanks do? Sit around and think, I suppose, but not about what's already at hand. They'd be thinking what if...what about...how can things be different? Imagination refers to the power of the mind to create images, and it is often linked to a vision, which is a spreading sense of something larger than what presently exists. A vision may contain nothing within it to suggest it could ever find legs, but coupled with the energy of imagination, ways and means begin to appear.

There is another side to the coin of imagination, and some say that this is worry. I think this is a good theory. It is naïve' to think that mental energy is always positive and forward thinking. Any worry wart can give you ten reasons why something can never happen, and some of their points are worth considering. It's not a question of being waylaid by negative thinking, it's a matter of covering all the possibilities and assessing them. If imagination misfires too often, we're liable to be reluctant to engage it. The very vital prosperity guru, Edwene Gaines, said that, regardless of how many academic degrees—or perhaps no degrees—we have earned, we all have letters after our names, to wit: M.S.U---Makes Stuff Up! We may all be smiling at this, but she was right. Imagination is not given only to Ph.D.'s or heads of corporations. Whoever and wherever we are, we can cook up stuff with the best of them! In fact I don't think the mental energy of imagination is necessarily heralded by the spreading of palm branches before every new idea we may get. Nor is everything we cook up worthy of the best of us.

Frankly, imagination is basically unstable. There can be nothing to lash it to an outcome, and we sometimes have no idea what we may be unleashing on the world. I think that the desired results of imagination come about through focused direction, and this can be like having a tiger by the tail. How do we take hold of the unbridled enthusiasms of a bright idea and neatly find its proper outlet? On the other hand, what happens when imagination has been negatively bent so long that it becomes habitually corrosive? It's one thing for enthusiasm to bring light to an idea and move it into action. It is quite another to be unaware that negative imagination is depressing action. It is difficult to get any steam going around the thought that "this will never work." Imagination is one of the great tools of the mind. In a way I think it's like a little kid. It needs to be free to expand and experiment, but I certainly wouldn't want to leave it alone too long.

On More Patience

In my last book, *Essays on Everything*, I wrote on Patience. I'm writing on it again. I'm haven't made enough ground; I'm not at the still place I want to be, at least not often enough, and I'm still making spaces for my own thoughts to come to me. There is no doubt in my mind that patience is not a natural, soul quality. It must be learned and practiced over time, more so these days perhaps because there is so much information that clamors for our attention. It is easy to pull out the iPhone and be inundated by the world at our doorsteps, and perhaps we have really come to like this, to never be shut off from news, messages, entertainment...and irritation.

The irritated mind cannot partake of the clarifying flow of patience; it does not think of one thing at a time and is always hurrying through an army of demands. If things are not occurring as we would wish, we are almost certain to be met with frustration, that quality of mind that fights with itself so that the mind takes to churning. No possibility for patience here. Irritation, frustration and patience simply cannot exist together in the same place at the same time. Let's not fool ourselves either by thinking that if we do not respond to a frustrating situation, we are being patient. For lack of a better word, I call this "reactive impatience," a silent appearance...perhaps well learned...that masks buried anger. Many of us just crush a rising inclination to boil into a response so that we can appear in control. It may indeed be some kind of control, but it is not patience. Real patience breeds health; the squelched response eventually breeds illness.

There really are just twenty four hours in a day. Are we pushing to fill them so full of stuff to do that we are grabbing for every breath? If we have come to this place, where the body can barely keep up, I think we're in trouble. My sainted mother, farm girl that she was, kept a very simple perspective about the situations before her. If undue stress was piling up in her life, she would have another "think" about things. This was her way of backing off from a situation loaded with confusion and sometimes heat. People always felt better being around her because of her calm demeanor. She was not disconnected from what was going on; she was one step away from it mentally so that she could see more clearly what needed attention... and what did not.

I think patience is borne of the opportunity to take another "think" about what is in front of us. Mentally we can do this; we can vacate the swirl in our minds and have a space for relief. It is difficult, especially if we are wired for impatience and worry. I cannot always find the patch of grace I need to take another "think," but I...and my patience...are still a work in progress.

On Kids

We are immersed in a world of children. Some are wanted; some come along by accident; some come through the birth process; some come through adoption; some are enchanting; some are difficult; some are ours; some are other people's children. In a word, we live surrounded by kids, and it is my belief that kids can never have too many people loving them. In fact they *need* as much love as they can possibly get, love that is patient, understanding and love that says no when it is needed.

Many kids live in what are called "broken" families; the unit is no longer intact and the members may become scattered. Some kids live in "blended" families, groups that did not begin together but come together as parents either remarry or form another family unit. I know something about this because I, a divorced woman with children, married a divorced man with children. I learned very quickly that these new kids are not "add-ons;" they are part of an entirely new family community. Challenging, yes! Rewarding, absolutely! And the ultimate magic comes about when the kids you have taken the time to love turn about and love *you*. Seems that we can never have enough kids loving us either!

When does a kid stop being a kid and become an adult? We all know the objective standards that indicate adulthood. That pliable little boy one day becomes surly and grows lots of hair. Our girls develop attitudes and wear clothes that seem way too tight. As adolescents they are on their way and will hopefully realize some of the guidelines we have given them until at last real adulthood emerges. I think that fathers delight in seeing their progeny grow up. Mothers, on the other hand, are another matter. They may be proud of their children's successes and may beam at Graduation Ceremonies or other celebratory recognitions, but in their hearts, those blossoming adults are still their kids. And even when those adults themselves begin to gray and change direction a time or two, they are still their kids. No one ever said that parenthood made perfect sense.

Then there is the second round of kids...grandkids, and these relationships can be a real head scratcher. If grandparents become responsible for raising grandkids, as sometimes happens, they have a second chance at correcting the mistakes they made the first time around and are often very diligent at it. On the other hand, if grandkids are being finely reared by their parents, grandparents can now attend to the ruination of grandkids by seriously spoiling them...and then giving them back at the end of the day! Go figure!

Admit it or not, kids are the extensions of our own lives. Certainly they will do what they choose to do, but a part of us goes with them, perhaps in a shared feature or a gesture. They may be lights of our lives or deep disappointments, but they are always in our hearts.

On Stress

About fifty years ago a Hungarian doctor named Hans Selye coined the word, stress, as a description of any external demands made on the body which provoked a response. By this standard, if I were sitting quietly and the phone rang, my response to answer it would be deemed a stress response. Simple enough, but over the last several decades our ideas of stress have expanded enormously. Dr. Selye himself helped with this expansion by making a distinction between stress and what he termed *distress*. According to him distress was a *negative* response to external demands, which gave it a lot more clout, and I guess we could say that the rest is history.

We are awash now in concerns about too much stress or, more accurately, distress. We are aware of illnesses due to stress, jobs that cause stress, stressful relationships, and medications for stress. Maybe we ourselves are among those who have heart problems due to stress, or skin rashes, body pain, you name it. Entire professions have been formed around the handling of stress. We understand now that people, things or situations that promote stress are called stressors. I think that even more important is the discovery that we now know we don't have to be tapped by something outside ourselves at all. We can stress ourselves to the max, endocrine glands cranked way up, by our own thoughts. Who would have thought that the activity of our own minds could be dangerous as well as inspiring?

There are books out now with titles like *Change Your Thinking, Change Your Life,* and we ought to pay attention to them or at least to their major ideas. Quite simply, if we continually spend time worrying extensively, being angry, frightened or upset, we will be pumping chemicals into the body systems that will make them work overtime. It doesn't take rocket science to figure out that undue illness and early death can likely result. And we'll need to figure out as well that the external world cannot help us. It will never calm down and be simple again, if, in fact, it ever was. Short of living in a convent or a monastery, we'll need to do our own settling. Simple, maybe, but not necessarily easy. We cannot ask of people what they cannot or will not do and expect to come away at peace. We cannot expect our bodies to be good partners if we keep them ginned up through constant mental irritation. Self care and genuine self love---which is not to be confused with conceit---are necessary for personal well being. I believe we really are the tenders of a calm mind, not other people, and what's more, we owe it to ourselves and all who love us to so tend. We need stimulation, of course, to get us off the couch and into action, but wisdom helps us to discern stimulation from inner assaults on the psyche. The world will always have its share of screaming meemies. Not a good idea to be one of them.

On It Is What It Is

'It is what it is.' How often have we spoken this glib set of words when viewing something in front of us that does not change, or perhaps cannot. They're a hopeless set of words, subjects and predicates that go nowhere. And, as we soon discover, 'it is what it is' always holds pain within its syllables... all the way from a dull, aching disappointment to a heart wound that takes time to close.

In my later years, after I had completed my pulpit work, I returned to university life to pursue an advanced degree. During this time I formed a very pleasant friendship with a professor that enabled us to spend good time together. She and I enjoyed conversations, lunches, e-mails and university meetings together which continued after I finished my studies. It was easy and effortless and included the gains and losses friends share as their lives march on. Then everything changed, almost from what seemed one day to the next. No more e-mails, no responses to any of my invitations, no answers to my queries. I hesitated to probe outside the limits of good taste, so after a silent year, I simply wrote a note speaking of my sadness that we seemed to have lost our connection. Eventually she wrote back, thanking me for "understanding," but making it clear that our time together was done.

What "understanding?", I thought. I understood nothing; I was clueless about what had changed. But then…quietly, almost without mercy, creeping into my unwilling awareness… 'it is what it is' appeared. I was not going to know why, and my only healthy choice was to let it all go. My western mind, which wanted reasons, fixes and nice, neat completions, was not going to get any. There would be no making peace, except within myself. 'It is what it is.'

These few words need to be part of our mental landscape, I think, for there are going to be instances that just will not line up. Some things will change, and we won't know why. And despite our best efforts and outpourings of love and energy some things will not change, and we won't know why. Some convergences are happy but seem not to last, despite our desires. Some convergences are unhappy and seem to last a lifetime, resisting healing at every turn. Once 'it is what it is' enters the picture, it can free us. Once it resounds in us securely and firmly, we are the ones who can change…and walk away. Sometimes we can literally leave a personal situation, and sometimes we are more closely bound to it, but in our minds and hearts we can give up the desire for an outcome we would have preferred. I think the love and energy seemingly given to no avail is not wasted because we come to know to what ends we are capable, and this knowledge is wonderful.

The wheel has turned; 'it is what it is'; time to move on.

On The Great Cactus Totem

Some biological wizardry has been taking place in our backyard lately. But first I should give the reader a sense of our lot so that this story will make sense. The lot is more than 200 feet long, and the parts closest to the house, front and back, we keep up. The way back, on the other hand, is more like an urban wilderness. We keep it cut down for safety and esthetic purposes, but don't pay it much more attention. Some twenty years ago someone gave us an agave' cactus which we promptly planted in the back area, out of our line of vision, and then proceeded to forget about. Now and again we would trek into the back of the yard and notice that the cactus seemed to be holding its own, actually a bit more than that. It was beginning to take up a lot of space and seemed somewhat threatening as it sported some pretty sharp spines. Fortunately it was a good distance from our activities.

A few months ago I checked the cactus out, only to find that it had grown to ten feet across and easily seven feet tall. This oversight, I decided, could only be called "inattention to detail." After this we all started paying attention to it, and like all things that are noticed, it responded. Within weeks it had sent up a stem that was eight inches in diameter and fifty feet tall. It was astounding! I took to calling it the Great Cactus Totem, and it would actually have looked like a thing to be worshipped if the stem had not looked so much like a humongous asparagus spear. Well, now all eyes were on the giant cactus. It was definitely no longer out of the line of sight but right in front of us as we looked out our deck windows.

Finally the stem stopped growing and started to unfurl very slowly, one patch at a time. We took to making up stories about what would come from it…small aliens perhaps, or maybe one, massive, all-consuming blossom. At last we could see the cactus' intentions. At the top ten feet of the stem, small, alternating arms-like protrusions began to extend themselves, some two feet long. At the end of each arm, a series of relatively tiny, white blossoms began to erupt. The very tip of the stem is still making up its mind, but I think it will culminate in one or two vertical thrusts of tiny blossoms. As a small person I have found this whole adventure in succulence quite daunting, and I'm a little afraid to get too close to the thing. (I actually did come a little too close once, and it bit me!)

Whenever I can I like to give meanings to things that occur, especially in the world of nature where growth and outcomes left alone can be quite exotic, as the cactus totem demonstrates. What comes to me easily, effortlessly and with a little smile as I watch our evolving giant in the backyard is…some things are simply worth the wait.

On The Cancer Experience

I am not a cancer survivor. I consider myself a post-cancer thriver, which may sound like a clumsy parsing of words. It isn't to me. It is the way I choose to think about a cancer experience I had over a dozen years ago. A routine medical examination indicated that I had uterine cancer; this was unexpected to say the least, and it took a good amount of mental integration for me to take it all in. Several emotions collided within me, fear, dismay (I had just entered into a course of study at a local university), concern about the upset to my family life. I did not resist the medical solution set before me, a complete hysterectomy, and I went into "training" for it, so to speak.

I took care of household and family needs, which was a godsend to my fragile state of mind. I walked; I took care of myself physically, and being a believer, mostly I prayed. None of this was a particular effort to me because of the way I do things. It was natural to put things in order; it was natural to enter more deeply into the spiritual practices I engaged in daily. Before me was a deal, but I hoped to make it no bigger than it had to be. Eventually the surgery came and went and was very successful...physically, mentally and emotionally.

After the experience, on my own time, I thought more carefully about the whole business. In my spiritual system, frames of thought influence our lives. We are not at the mercy of events that come and go; we participate in them and can control much of what we want to experience. Using this logic I could and did ask: Did I cause this cancer? I didn't really know. Did I participate in some way? Very likely, but I decided not to remain in regrets around such a possible lapse in good thinking. Instead I decided to make sure my Infinite connections and thought processes were clearer than ever.

I think that when threats pass through our lives, questions will always come. Did I dodge a bullet? Did I get lucky? Did God love me more than others who did not survive physically? These thoughts made no sense to me. They only created confusion when clarity was needed. Not all things resolve themselves into plain facts, and I was not going to waste time trying to find reasons for everything. Anyone who has experienced cancer of some sort casts an occasional, side-long look at the beast in the corner. We always know in a quiet place in our minds that it could come back. Not to acknowledge this is to throw fairy dust around, but no one said we needed to stare obsessively at the beast either. I think that wisdom and love would have us live our lives with as much equanimity as we can, weighing possibilities but not losing our balance either. I never claimed the cancer as "my" cancer. It was an episode like many others that was a part of my experience. It opened me, but it did not define me. It was a part of the history that added to who I am. I did not welcome it, and I did not despise it either. I accepted it...and moved on.

On God

I am a believer. Not perhaps in the ways that some people are, but I came into life knowing I belonged to something greater than myself. Never had to think about it or even ask questions. I just always knew it was there...or maybe I should more correctly say it was *here*. In fact I didn't know how to think about my place in the larger picture until I discovered a composed, spiritual system that helped me put my thoughts together. With a good spiritual foundation under my belt, I have been able to think rationally about my connection to the universe and also to know that reason could only get me part of the way. There had to be a place for intuitive awareness that operates outside the realm of reason, the place of faith, belief and inspiration, the openness to love.

Many of us seek God using many names. 20th Century German philosopher, Karl Jasper, had his *existenz*; his countryman before him, G.W.F. Hegel, wrote of the Historical Spirit spilling into time and space...and Victor was intimate with "Johnny." Let me explain. As a young, WWII pilot flying for the RAF, my husband had the sense of something "whispering in his ear," so to speak, as he pursued German Messerschmitts in his tiny aircraft. This "something" he called Johnny, not realizing then that he was touching a link to the largeness of life. And it appeared that God is not much concerned about what names we use either!

So often the great thinkers have tried to prove the existence of an Infinite Spirit, but God is not a fact and should not be treated as such. In his search St. Thomas Aquinas created Five Proofs of God, but I don't think of them as proofs; I find them mostly rational projections based on the Grand Assumption that a god exists. Proofs of God do not lie in pragmatic postulations; they do not lie in books, great sayings or the words of theologians. They lie in the heart of the believer, not as static edicts but as a moving flow of thoughts and experiences...sometimes uncertain. We just cannot put our finger on a divine certainty that will please everyone, and maybe we should stop trying.

Perhaps we should concentrate more on the idea that if a pristine being exists with which we are intimately connected, how would we live to better reflect this? We may not have all the whys and hows sorted out, but what if there is a greater part of ourselves that informs our thoughts and actions? Do the ways in which we live our lives reveal this, and what better forms of worship could there be than if they did? Could there be a worse form of blasphemy than to engage in killing in the name of God? Surely there can be no holiness in holy wars.

The philosopher, Ernest Holmes, in a moment of whimsy once said, "Thank God, the God believed in, isn't!" Perhaps we could return to our churches, temples, mosques, gurdwaras, sanghas and simple quiet places once more to make the inner discovery, maybe for the first time.

On Ordinary Miracles

To a lot of people, miracles mean something completely unnatural, like setting aside the laws of nature to allow someone to fall out of a three-story window and hit the ground unharmed. Or maybe being able to stave off the inevitable consequences of some unfortunate act we may have initiated. As far as I am concerned, sometimes getting out of bed in the morning is a miracle. Oy! (Bones don't always want to cooperate much!) Seriously, though, miracles do not have to be big, earth-shattering deals; they can be and often are the most effortless flows in the world. In fact I think that the definition of a miracle can be reduced to five, simple words: The truth revealed without obstruction.

There is a spiritual portent to this that does not involve a god that rearranges the laws of the universe to satisfy our needs. I am not talking about a god that stops a lava flow in mid descent because we choose to live at the foot of an active volcano. As I have often written, I am a believer, and I revere the deep, abiding connection that is always present among all of life, however we may postulate this. I believe as the ancients said that I live, move and have my being in something greater than myself. Some days...no lights, bells and whistles...some days...a bird song or two outside the window...or maybe a bit more.

Does it deflate the whole idea of miracles to deem them so simple? Oh, sometimes they come as flashy whiz bangs, as something that occurs that is big and magnificent like a wonderful, unexpected healing. But I also think that healings of any kind would always be possible if we could clear up our infernal capacities to misunderstand everything! This, friends, would truly be a miracle! No kidding, it would be because we finally share the awareness of our connections with the great love and wisdom of That Within Which we all live and move. There are no pragmatic proofs of the miracle maker, only those that come as light through minds and hearts. No books, no gurus can give us what we can only know and experience for ourselves, and every wonder will not line up according to reason. Once we are open to this and don't disparage what we can't always explain, we are ready for ordinary miracles...things that fall into place just as they should...our being exactly where we need to be...large and small gifts coming to us...bringing gifts we never knew we had.

Ordinary miracles would follow our footsteps every day if we would let them, and in fact they often do. When we get out of the way of our own truths, they come forth as the most natural things in the world. How can we not know this? Probably because we don't always know how to look. What if we woke up one morning with a dawning clarity about something we had been wrestling with for God knows how long? If that isn't a sweet miracle, I don't know what is!

On Doing Nothing

Many years ago when my son was a small boy, we had a large, overstuffed chair that backed up to a bay window. It framed a wonderful view, for we could see the city of San Francisco, the bay and the headlands of a small, North Bay community. Often I would come from another part of the house and find my son sitting on the shoulders of the chair, gazing quietly out the window. He could sit there calmly for as long as an hour if he had nothing required of him and not say a word the entire time. Once I asked him what he was doing, and he simply replied, "nothing," without averting his gaze. I knew enough not to probe his stance but to just leave him alone until he easily hopped off his perch and went on to something else.

He never spoke of his sittings, and I could not help but wonder what was taking place. What did his nothing involve? Was he turning over a problem? Was he upset about something (although he did not seem to be)? Or was he just as Walt

Whitman once wrote, "inviting his soul"? I remember those days as less complicated than at other times in the life of our family, so perhaps it was possible for him to let himself simply be and take in the refreshing quiet. If I were to ask him now, whiskery as he is, if he remembers that time, I'm sure he would, and he might even share a retrospective on it now that time has distanced him from it. The episodes were gifts to him, I'm sure of that, and perhaps he knows that also.

These days doing nothing hardly seems an option any more. Technology allows us to cram our days with more activity than ever, although the value of doing so can often seem questionable. I know a lot of people who find themselves in a whole lot of overwhelm, and they are not coping all that well. Consequently we might want to reconsider the value of doing nothing on a regular basis. How much time has gone by since we just hung out with ourselves long enough for stuff to come to us? Some of the best ideas tend to show up when there is an open place in the mind that allows for a little, mental adventure. Our most important, inner needs haven't changed. We may be able to respond more quickly to what is demanded, but we still need time to do...nothing.

It may be a little difficult to find a chair with big shoulders to sit on, but there are good alternatives...maybe a bean bag chair in which we could lose ourselves for awhile. Just so we don't forget how.

On The Color Red

I think we all have certain basics with which we came into life. There are certain chords or characteristics that resonate with us that we may know nothing about until they begin to erupt into little knowings that we can recognize. As silly as this may seem, for me one of these is the color red. Red may not seem like much, especially to non-red lovers, but when someone becomes all alight when red enters the picture, you just can't ignore this. From the very first, when I began to distinguish colors, red called my name. Red shouted at me; red had me in its grip. Although I am fond of many colors, I can't even imagine what might come second. Red ranks right up there with chocolate, which you can read about in my book, Essays on Everything. This love fest around a color may seem a bit nutty but it serves to remind us that the basic importances in us should not be overlooked, and there are of course more defining basics than red and chocolate...might not be as much fun, but way more telling in our lives.

Once we begin the learning process these basics begin to show up, even if they are inchoate at first. We aren't born as moral beings, for instance, but as we are taught moralities some pop up as if they were waiting to be discovered. For some, learning to tell the truth will be as basic as eating and drinking. For others, lies will always come easily to their lips, and truth telling will be an effort. The business of learning about ourselves is never easy, and there can be a fine line to delineate what civilizes us and what inspires us. If we are lucky, they work well together and give our energies a fine alignment. At other times we may fight with what we want to do and what is "right" to do. This can be very tricky business. We cannot always dismiss the "right" as some artificial imposition on us when it calls to the highest senses of our humanity. It is just too bad that our choices cannot always be as simple as deciding on a favorite color.

Still, we can always be working on the best of ourselves all the times, even when that "best" isn't having a very good day. This is part of our humanity at work, self correcting as we go along. I believe we grow up all our lives and work with our basic core right along. Even control freaks come to know they can't control everything, and that people are not going to do what they would like them to do. It should be obvious that setting up armed camps against people we don't like will not get us where we want to go either.

I fear life will never be as simple as choosing the color red. If I had my way, hens would lay red eggs; the night stars would be twinkling red; our cash money would go from light red to dark red, depending on the denominations of the bills.......

See what I mean.

On Taking Risks

Life is a risky business; everyone knows this, especially since the media constantly thrusts tragedy and loss at us through all available sources. I thought that maybe it's time to take a look at what living in the world today can mean. Each morning as we go out the front door, there is no guarantee we will come back through it at the end of the day. And it gets even riskier, depending on the kinds of choices we make in the course of the day. Being a bicycle courier involves braving the wilds of city traffic; sending an e-mail doesn't. I'm for the latter, but some people may be really stimulated by the former. Nevertheless unless we are highly neurotic and are paralyzed in place by our fears, we will take risks. We will venture into what the day holds and make the best of it.

I guess we could look at some risk categories here. In other words, what turns us on? What makes someone want to stick his neck out and generate the obvious discomfort in doing so? I know one thing: Risk of any kind tends to make us feel more alive. Certain brain chemicals get cranked up and send out all kinds of feel good signals. There is the "go do it" place in us that rears its head a lot when we are younger and then, if we're not careful, tends to soften all the rough edges. Maybe that's not such a good idea. Maybe we need a few rough edges around to keep us curious about what lies around the corner.

We get to know ourselves over time. We know the calm places, the scary places and the complacent places in us. We know the beyond-which-I-will-not-go places and the I-wonder-what's-over-there places. These are not necessarily based on fear either. Sometimes we're just not that curious. I have no interest in strapping myself behind Mario Andretti in a race car, but I would consider looking into a belief system that is completely foreign to me. These choices are not as obvious as they look. I think I would trust the skill of Mario Andretti enough to jump in behind him and get rattled to pieces. I might, on the other hand, check out some mental system or guru that could freak me out completely. What I am saying is that all physical choices are not necessarily that destabilizing, nor are the adventures of the mind that safe.

Perhaps it comes down to asking ourselves how much of the unknown we are willing to explore. And are we simply looking for another adrenaline rush? There is no sin in being joyful and satisfied in the place in which we find ourselves. There is only the concern that we may button down our minds a little too tightly. Maybe we need a little air sometimes. Or we can get so addicted to being physically stimulated that we can find ourselves unable to enjoy the quiet. Possibly we could ask ourselves what kind of risks we *should* be taking. What stretch do I need to take to be true to my own well being? The other side of this coin holds another question. Can I know when to stay put right where I am? This is, of course, a moveable feast and can change at any time, so we will need to pay attention to where we find ourselves.

On Being the Best We Can Be

The comparison game is a losing proposition, even though one of the easiest ways to feel "up" is to put someone else "down." But this doesn't last forever. Sooner or later another person will come along playing the same game more successfully, and we will be on the losing end of things. Besides it's a tenuous thing trying to make ourselves seem better by playing off making another seem worse. Often these scenarios turn out to be total inventions, some mental construct that is a mind game, something we made up to be all right with ourselves.

This is a lonely path, and we usually have to keep running to stay ahead of the game. Along the way, do we ever stop running long enough to see what's going on? Do we know that in the running there is little notice of our being a real person or discovering just what we are capable of doing in the course of our lives? I think that this comes from a fear that we are "not enough…" never good enough at being ourselves. Actually this is a wonderful time to be alive, especially for those of us who are unsure about ourselves. Diversity is flourishing, and self discovery could not be more highly prized. Seminars and communal meetings are springing up everywhere to assist people in valuing the unique persons that they are. Now we are all encouraged to be the best that we can be.

Not only is this a noble, spiritual goal, it is pragmatic wisdom as well. When we are not functioning from a sense of best-ness, we are wasting time and energy, and most likely we're performing in an underlying maze of dissatisfaction. We know we can do more and better, which has nothing to do with what someone else is doing. Here is where the comparison game fails. Our best-ness is not concerned with someone else's best or worst. It involves the goals and standards we set for ourselves. Since there are only a few prizes in competitions, if we do not win one, does this somehow mean we are not performing at a level of our highest excellences? Are our gifts and efforts unworthy? We know this thinking does not make sense. If we took away prize giving and simply let people exhibit their skills and talents, all of us spectators would be absolutely overwhelmed at the splendid choices before us, all magnificent, all unique, all different. There would be outrageous beauty for all to take away, for none would be lacking.

If we are giving our best shot at whatever we are doing, everybody wins. Certainly we the doers are more lively and clearer than ever, even if our efforts are not the flashier arts. There is great goodness and pleasure in being on hand when someone does his or her finest. The doer cannot miss it, nor can the observer. It is as if we are all more fully engaging the greater good in which we live and move and cannot fail to be lifted by the acts of giving and receiving.

On Letting Go

The whole idea of letting go is not new. One of the great practices of the mind involves an agreement to stop wrestling with the unyielding situation lying in front of us and just let it go. Right release is a part of healthy thinking, and most anyone who follows a mental/spiritual system knows it. In fact sooner or later anyone who has been banging his head against the wall long enough will finally stop out of sheer exhaustion. Reason would tell us that release has now freed us, and we are good to move forward to something newer...yes? If clear thinking and wisdom prevail, certainly this would be so, but more often than not, this is not so. Instead, we will get a second wind, hang on and take another run.

The human animal is a strange beast. Our animal brothers and sisters in nature know when to let go. We're all familiar with documentaries on animal behaviors, some showing us an ape mother carrying around a dead infant, for instance. Because of these films we now know that our closest relatives in the animal world, the great apes, experience grief and emotion, especially over loss. We have watched them gather around an infant carcass, perhaps wondering why it will not rise, but eventually leaving it to the elements and moving on. They can and do experience a final letting go. We, on the other hand, often will not. We will carry dead things around with us endlessly...a lost relationship, jobs that did not work out, children that went on to terrifying choices.

There is no question that some of these outcomes are very serious and cannot be trivialized. What, for instance, does a parent do when a child commits a terrible crime that involves a lifetime in prison? How does a mother square up such a thing in her own mind? What if it seems impossible to do so? All the love in the world may never bring that child physical freedom, and what's worse, what if that parent becomes so consumed that she finds herself in a prison without bars, unable to let go and move forward?

Hopefully we may never find ourselves in such an outrageous position, but we can become stuck behind invisible bars that we are not even noticing. Some things may never resolve to our liking, and we will have to let go for our own health's sake. There is no question that it takes courage to let some person or circumstance go to whatever they will become. Release is always a choice, from the simplest to the most difficult, but behind the decision to release, there is light...broad, expanding, vibrant light, starting as a tiny pinprick perhaps, but unfailingly opening toward us. There may be places of remembered sorrow that tell us of the thing that would not heal, but life's natural light beckons. It always does. It always will when we let go. There is a magic in this that reason cannot fathom, and maybe it isn't necessary that it does.

On Cooking a Frog

I love to use little metaphors to make a point, and there is a story these days that creates a very obvious image. To wit: If you toss a frog into a pot of boiling water, it will hop out immediately. On the other hand, if you toss a frog into a pot of cool water and turn on the fire, it will slowly get used to the increasing temperature and eventually let itself boil to death. Grim story, but it makes an unmistakable point. It illustrates serious inattention. In fact if I wanted to give this essay a different title, I would call it "On Not Paying Attention." Our lives can move along, seemingly in a particular direction, and then end up where we had never meant to go. We can be asking ourselves the question, "How did I get here?", and then search for the answer. Often we will find a series of unnoticed choices...or non choices...that brought us where we are.

It is Socrates who said that "the unexamined life is not worth living." While I would hardly go that far, I would say that an unexamined life can cause us to be caught in a drift we hadn't noticed. I could also call this essay, "On Thinking Ahead," so that we might be able to avoid some of the hot water into which we get ourselves.

It is true that some of us plan our lives down to the last detail, almost ad nauseum sometimes. Nice work if you can get it and not be interrupted by wars, pestilences, family trauma or simply, the unexpected. Many things can interrupt the most thoughtful plan, but a heartfelt way to go can still carry a vision when the smoke clears enough for clarity to emerge. Some of us end up in quite different places than we had imagined, but the original heart's desire does not necessarily go astray. Can we not also do what we had in mind in another venue?

I believe there is a general guiding principle that runs through all and this is to express life fully. We can do this in a gazillion different ways, but we will need to pay attention to it. Nature finds ways to express itself because it knows nothing else. The creeper blocked off by a wall will go through a crack or extend its tendrils around the wall. You and I can sigh and forget the whole thing. Not important enough, I guess...or maybe it is, but we simply stop seeking other ways to be fulfilled. We don't have to handle everything that comes along. Maybe it really is not that important, but we don't have to be casual about it either. There are always choices in front of us, and the mind is always thinking because, unless insanity clouds it permanently, it can't do otherwise. Barring the inability to think clearly, we will need to keep noticing and deciding. We can be directive or give our lives over to fate, and that would truly be the tragedy.

On Doing What is Ours to do

I have often said laughingly that if I could, I would pay other people to exercise for me! I am not physically athletic, and I really dislike doing the sweatier things in life. Nevertheless I have fended off the ravages of arthritis for years by assiduously engaging in a mild, necessary exercise regimen to keep from seizing up into debilitating stiffness. Why? Because this is mine to do. Whether we planned on them or not, there are going to be things that are ours to do.

I do not subscribe to the idea that we are responsible for everything that happens to us. To my colleagues in spiritual work, such a thought would be heresy; it would be viewed as vacating our self responsibilities. Not so. I am not suggesting that we are not a part of the things of our lives. I am only saying that we are involved in such a complicated mix of life in our shared oneness that we cannot have initiated every piece of it. Having said this, I also add that once we recognize the strength of our spirituality, we can get busy doing what is ours to do and knowing that spirituality is involved in every bit. Can I, for instance, decide that some things are spiritual and some are not? I never imagined that doing knee bends was an element of my spiritual practices, but they are. They are mine to perform.

If we want to think of ourselves as responsible, spiritual beings leaving footprints on the ground, there are things, acts and choices that belong to us. If we have become parents, either by choice or carelessness, it is ours to see our children raised in the best possible ways. If we have chosen to love others, it is ours to let them be who they are without trying to remake them to our satisfactions. If we have something or someone that needs forgiveness, it is ours to forgive and also release ourselves and the others into freedom, which is the last piece of forgiveness.

Doing what is ours to do as self-aware individuals is not easy. Self awareness in its essence means giving up the self delusions we may have created to make ourselves feel right and others feel wrong. There may be some self-defeating habits we have to give up so that we can live into real, self knowledge. It took a while for me to admit that coach potatohood was not going to allow me to stay physically flexible. No one likes pain, but it can be a powerful driver. And there is real power in doing what is ours to do. What do "wake-up calls" mean if not seeing more clearly what belongs to us? If we thought about it a little more, we might see that the individual gifts we have to bring to life, little and large, are probably the holiest of all the things that are ours to give. This is not insignificant. I believe it is a prime fulfillment of ourselves.

On Mindfulness

Buddhism, in its wisdom, has given us an ethical, pragmatic path to follow as we attempt to live good lives. As other worldly as Buddhism sometimes can seem to be, this path appears surprisingly sensible, and its footprints contain right views, intentions, speech, conduct, livelihood, effort, mindfulness and concentration. Other nouns can be used but they all essentially point to thoughtful, directive, worthwhile ways to live a blessed life. Most seem obvious to me...I know what it means to speak kindly and lovingly, for instance...but the quality that gets my attention is *mindfulness*, a deep exploration that goes beyond the word itself.

What is it to be mindful? Does being mindful mean keeping the mind occupied with all sorts of habits and subjective content, or does it mean a mind that is emptied of unnecessary baggage? I would think that a successful mentality involves a thinker who can wheel and turn quickly, someone who is alert enough to catch the movement of the Divine and be moved along with it to enlightened thinking. Perhaps being mindful actually involves "lean and mean" thinking, the ability to view all things in new ways, not getting bogged down in the constraints of old-time structures. Treasured principles are to be revered and kept alive, and by the same token, not muddied by more talk than practice.

There is a freedom to be found in mindfulness. One of the nouns used in place of mindfulness is right meditation, which has always meant an openness to the Divine channels, as far as I am concerned. When one meditates, he or she may use a directive practice to get into meditation, but once in that open place, all kinds of freshness may breeze into the mind, bringing new mental expansions. The beauty of meditation is the newness that always accompanies it, for no two meditative sessions are ever the same.

In mindfulness we can approach the Changeless with an openness to change. Does this seem enigmatic, just playing with words? I think not. We take a very small cup with us when we go exploring the waters of Mind, so we are bound to take away a different draft at each foray. I think there is excitement in this. We're looking at a journey of constant discovery, sometimes quieting and calming...especially if we ask for it...sometimes a bit unsettling if a new, spiritual horizon appears before us.

Perhaps adventurousness might be another good noun to use in place of mindfulness. Certainly we long for assurances of belonging to something greater than ourselves, and I think we enter into mindfulness with this desire. However we cannot ask that our experiences not take us into wild country. Sometimes they will, and we'll just have to not mind this...maybe antic-ipate it a bit. We are taking a great spiritual sojourn for the long haul, sometimes not staying in one place too long, and the roads will take us to many awarenesses. It is mindfulness that opens the doors and sets out the light.

On Grace

Grace can mean a lot of things. Aside from being a lovely, feminine name, it can be viewed as a divine dispensation. The "grace of God" usually refers to a divine gift given to the undeserving, something that God gives even though we, the receivers, may not merit it (which, incidentally, I do not buy. I think of God as essential being that is revealing itself through creation, not making choices as to who gets and who doesn't. This, however, is a topic for another essay.)

Then there is the "grace of beautiful movement." We are very aware of some living things, maybe human beings, maybe some animals, who strike our senses with the fluidity and ease of their physical movements. They seem to track from one place to another with a minimum of thought, effort and no impediments to their travel. At the very least they are a joy to watch.

There is also what I like to call the "grace of small deals," which some people carry off with aplomb. At any time during a busy day things can unravel and go awry; emergencies can pop up; people can be freaking out about any number of things, and still those possessing the grace of small deals can move through all of these without ever letting anything turn into a big deal. It is not that he or she of the small deal minimizes or makes less important the very important. It is that there seems to be in such people the quiet, strong, stabilizing ability to keep hysterical behaviors from erupting. By their very presence they are a settling influence. It cannot be said that they are without feelings because this makes no sense. Everyone is subject to the emotion inherent in a situation. None of us live outside the moment in some kind of vacuum.

I think that small-deal people, those who are full of grace, carry with them a sense of their own place in life. Perhaps it can be said that they know themselves, that they have real love for themselves and that they know they are loved by others. Frankly I think that firefighters can be full of grace. Whenever I see depictions of them engaging in their tasks, they seem to be little-dealing whatever is happening. No doubt there is excitement and a sense of urgency in what they do. No question either that they can be putting themselves in harm's way, but their disciplines in handling what lies before them appear to be an almost choreographed flow. One cannot help but be inspired at the sight of them in action.

Perhaps it could be said that those who have a real sense of self and the discipline that goes with directing that self are naturally full of grace. They can be very young...some little children meander along, enjoying their own sphere. They can be very old...some elderly folks know how to stand comfortably wherever they find themselves.

Whenever I see the grace-filled, I am transfixed by them. I don't envy them. I would simply like to be one of them.

On a Generous Spirit

I know a man who can only be called a generous spirit. I say this because there is no withholding of anything in him, no second thoughts, no hesitations, only full-on intentions to bring himself into any situation before him. Not that he thinks about this. I never sense calculations going on in his brain nor real distaste if there are messes to clear up. I just see a guy who really likes being a friend and family member. He doesn't have money to burn, and he never seems to long for things that are outside his price range. He is quite able to make the things of his life work and adds a charm to all of it.

When he cooks, he cooks for an army, and he is never stingy with anything. When he takes care of his three-year-old granddaughter, he dotes on her. When he worries about his adult children, he worries from every pore, but they'll never know it. As a little boy, when his mother would scold him, he'd tease her into laughing before all was done. Once, in his sweetness, he wrote her a note saying, "I love you, even if you make me take out the garbage."

Is this a bit of biography that will alter the course of the planets in their orbits? Hardly. Is it one that would gladden the hearts of parents and friends everywhere? Absolutely! There are so many intrusions into our daily lives that it can be hard to find a place to rest, to find renewal and quiet. I think it is a gift to be able to hang our hats around people who bring their natural cheer into their tasks. If I want to learn more arcane knowledge, I'll take a course at a college somewhere. If I want to be upset and excited, I'll turn on cable news. If I want opinions on everything, I'll stand with the ladies in a church kitchen. I know how to get myself worked up.

However I think there is a place of health and wholeness in us that needs attention and care, and we cannot always trust ourselves to mind that store. Demands and desires tend to run our days, often from dawn way into the evening. We may even tell ourselves that we'll slow down, but I have discovered that most people don't, even if they could. It is just too tempting to stick another task into an open space. But just let a generous spirit loose among us...let a generous spirit sail into the room, and everything seems to settle down. They always bring gifts, not necessarily something substantial, but often a small token from their hearts...maybe a cup of hot coffee or a silly, little story.

In all the measures of what we think a man should be, I think the generous-spirited one should have a gold star after his name. It takes courage as well as self awareness to bear gifts to others and ask for nothing in return.

On Giving and Receiving

There is a school of thought that examines the concept of giving and receiving, which can involve the giving and receiving of money, but often considers the giving and receiving of ideas and more often, the *thinking* about giving and receiving. Is it clear? Is it generous? Is it fearful, constrained, full of unwillingness, etc? In spiritual studies we would be looking at the Law of Cause and Effect, which deals with the nature of what we are thinking and doing and the logical outcomes of what we have sent forth.

It appears there is nothing we can send out, in thought or in action that does not return to us pretty much in kind. This is not a Law we made up; this is something we discovered at a universal level as we participated in the come and go of life itself. If we do not know about this natural activity, it can get quite frightening finding all kinds of unexpected conditions at our doorsteps with no idea how they got there. But if we are aware of the sacred connection we have with the universe itself, we will know that our participation in it does not go without consequences. If we, then, ill use the Law of Cause and Effect, we will find lots of nasty surprises.

This does not have to work at a big deal level either. We may have already discovered that the way we think about and consequently act on things will bring about what we expect. If we go forth with a bad attitude, we will find other bad attitudes to meet us. It is folly to think that we will find sweetness and light in return for curt, rude comments. Ernest Holmes wrote that we cannot expect to gather roses from thistles. This is a no brainer, but our mental activity can be a lot more subtle... underground we might think, never surfacing into overt thought or physical activity we might think. Still the nature of our mental storage will not remain hidden; it will emerge in some way. As a rule it is not life-affirming storage that is a problem. We don't much hide what we love; we give it forth and receive outcomes that are positive and encouraging. It is the quiet mindsets of anger and negativity that contain poisons that work their ways out into our lives.

At the end of the day we keep no secrets, which is a scary thought indeed. Others may not know book, chapter and verse what is going on inside us, but they know something is up. The lover who has just asked his sweetheart to marry him and received a positive response carries a look of great joy that beams out of him before he says a word to anyone. By the same token, someone who is carrying deep anger or guilt around will find it written in his face and body for all to notice.

I believe we are spiritual beings, everyone, from which there is no abdication. We move in the action of the Infinite, whether we know it or not. We had really better come to know the power fulminating inside us...and use it well.

On The Golden Silence

The person who said that "silence is golden" definitely knew what he was talking about, and initially he was probably an ancient Egyptian. Seems that this favorite has been with us longer than we might have thought. Somewhere along the way another addition to that statement sometimes shows up to tell us that "speech is silver and silence is golden," suggesting that while conversation brings us things of importance, silence can be even more valuable.

No surprise in this. Our days can be filled with words coming from every direction, so much so that it can feel as if every quiet place is squeezed out of us. In fact we can become so used to the clatter of talk or ambient sounds that, if a sudden silence breaks through, we almost don't know what to do. Sometimes we even rush to fill the quiet spot. If we get into these awkward stretches, it can tell us that we are out of touch with our inner lives. We are caught in Shakespeare's "sound and fury" and don't know what to do without it.

Spiritual practices involve a lot of silence. There can indeed be movement that accompanies the silence, but in the quiet is where self awareness surfaces. How can we really come to ourselves if there is not a space where our own thoughts may be made available to us? Some speak of the "monkey mind," the head chatter that runs through our minds at a surface level, so full of stories, so pervasive that original thinking has a hard time of it. We are not helped by this inner noise. It drowns out emerging originality that is still vulnerable in its infancy.

Believers think that we use the Infinite Mind as the foundation of all thought, both manifest and unmanifest. I believe that there is a treasure trove of information and inspiration that is available to us through the annals of Mind, but this needs a means of making its way to our private consciousness. One of the surest and best paths is through silence, when competing, ground-level wrangling is set aside for awhile at least, and we become better receivers. Not everything comes as a thunderclap to the mind, pushing its way through great activity. Often some of the most precious gems come quietly and gradually, forming in our thoughts even as we track through the day or rest in sleep at night.

As geared as the human is for activity, as cosmologist, Ernest Holmes, has said, it is good to know when to practice perfect inaction. As a species we need managed doses of reflection and action. A self-regulated silence lets all kinds of healing streams move as a stabilizing, calming, thoughtful essence within the thinker. External noises can be de-stabilizing and unnerving, but more so is the mind that thrashes around in its negative histories, fears and angers. How valuable, then, would be the silence that heals and reveals!

On Old Friends

I have been around long enough now to have created a history of my own. I have lived through many events, long enough to have gained a thing called perspective, something that most young people don't yet know about. The teenager whose girl friend leaves him thinks he will never get over it and never love again. I know different. I know that it won't be too long before another flashing smile will catch his eye. He just does not yet know that pain does heal and memories dim.

Time, people and circumstances come and go, but not in a meaningless stream. There are those times, those people and those circumstances that make an impact on the heart and memory that can never be replaced. Old friends are like that. I always look forward to what new introductions can bring... such as a new baby or a new job...but when I am looking for assurances and a place to lay back, I go to old friends.

Some of the wonderful oldies are no longer with me in the flesh, but our times and exploits together are a part of the growing up that has made me who I am. I think of a good, reliable friend (still with me, blessedly) who has walked with me through many of the highs and lows of my life...deaths, losses, divorce...always bringing her gift of non-judgmentalness. At one time when I was very unsure of myself and my choices, I turned to her tentatively, probably looking for approval, and her steady tone told me, "I love you, and whatever you do is ok with me." Nothing replaces good underpinnings like that.

The mind holds old friends for us as well, if we will think back a bit. No doubt there are ways of thinking and behaving that may no longer serve us; hopefully these we will have jettisoned, but values we have learned and practiced remain as mental foundations. When did we discover that others are as deserving of the good things of life as we are? What wise person showed us that an adversarial stance accomplishes only disagreement and inevitable push-back?

Of course there are always newer and faster ways to accomplish our desires, but do they sometimes leave out the humility and humanity that are vital and precious to us? It is very easy in the world of new means to overlay the old importances as no longer meaningful. If we fall heir to this we have ceased to be as picky as we should be about the care of old friends of the mind. We live in the midst of thunder every day, loud and noisy ideas that vie for our attention and would make irrelevant that which went before, but maybe not always worthy of too much

attention. T.S. Eliot wrote that "we shall not cease from exploration, and at the end of our exploring will be to arrive where
we started and know the place for the first time"...old friends
made new again.

On Shoes

I love shoes…always have, and anyone who has known me for a while knows this. I think shoes are a part of my spiritual DNA because the lure they hold for me is unmistakable. At one time whenever I passed a display of elegant shoes, I could swear I heard an unearthly voice whispering to me, "Buy me!", and I wasn't always able…or willing…to resist its siren call. It all began when I was a young teenager and bought my first pair of high heels…four-inch platforms, black patent leather, open toes with ankle straps. I wore them all day until my feet almost fell off. From then on I was hooked. Believe me, if my veteran hips and ankles could hold me up, I'd have a pair of the new, killer five inchers right now!

There was a good reason for my love of these babies. Shoes were my fancy place. Wearing feathered stitching on the seams and metal fittings around the toes, I would toss my head, kick up my heels and say to myself, "Watch me!", as I stepped into what that time of my life held for me. It was exciting; it was wonderful...and it was then. Oh, I still love shoes, and I can feel the old beckoning whenever I pass an array of beautiful footwear, but they are not my fancy place any more. When I step out into what this time of my life has for me, it is no longer nifty shoes that carry me along, partly because my body can no longer handle the height and imbalance of super shoes, partly because I am not a mono-pronged person. I find that there is not only one way to create life situations but many means available, some of which I had not imagined in my shoe years.

I think that all of us have had a fancy place in us some-where, not like mine perhaps, but a place we could count on when we participated in our own lives. It might have been an exciting place, a comfortable place or maybe a goad that pro-voked an uncomfortable jab to get us going. Whatever that place was, sooner or later it did not fit the growing human being that we were becoming. We had to step out of it. We can always love it for what it has meant to us. Whether it was dif-ficult or friendly, it helped bring us to where we are. Still there are other openings, other places that are ours to follow, and we deny them at our peril. A single-eyed approach can create stuckness when it goes on too long.

There can be fear, yes, and it need not keep us in one place. Fear has its value. It tells us that something before us needs our attention, and we are not yet willing to give it. We will, though, because the shoes may be just too tight now. Nevertheless I keep a pair of the fancies in the back of my closet...for old times' sake.

On Doubt

About one thing I have no doubt...and that is that I will doubt. At one time in my foolish youth I believed there would be a time when I would be so certain of myself and what I know that I would be doubt free. Looking back I now say to myself... how silly was that! In fact I had a wonderful old friend who said, "to doubt is the beginning of wisdom." She was so right. I think she understood that doubt-free people usually engage in my-way-or-the-highway thinking. Their certainty was more curse than blessing since there was no room for shared opinions...or growth, which usually accompanies uncertainty.

Doubt tells us we're alive. The 17th Century French philosopher, Rene' Descartes, is known for his famous *cogito ergo sum*: I think therefore I am. He could just as well have said, "I *doubt* therefore I am." Doubt and complacency just do not exist in the same space; the complacent person does not ask questions; the doubtful person is full of them. Often some think that some kind of weakness is associated with people who experience lack of certitude. I think that this is really unfortunate since uncertainty is often the way into new awareness. Any of us who have explored religious or spiritual systems surely have come across this. The look into something that cannot be quantified, weighed, measured or completely rationalized...which is usually true of queries into belief systems...is found to be overlaid with elements that cannot really be factually verified. The believer chooses to believe, even though he cannot prove his inner experiences nor transfer them to another person. I think that enough personal, spiritual senses over time and practice enable the believer to live with the glimmers of doubt that can arise. He makes his peace with the god that does not perform on cue and moves into hundreds of little assurances that can almost go unnoticed. When dealing with what cannot be fully known, one has to learn how to pay attention!

Are there any real certainties that we can count on? I think so, as long as we are not asking people or situations to do what we want them to do. I, for instance, have no doubt that my family loves me. We have grown through a lot of difficult situations, and we are all still willingly on scene. I do doubt that they always *like* me at times since I am still infected with the parental disease called intrusiveness. I do meddle in their lives. Fortunately they are wise, forgiving and know how to love. I do not doubt this.

As it turns out, a little island of certainty can go a long way in navigating a sea of doubtful situations. Love is one of these islands. Self love is the most durable, but a few folks at our sides along the way make for a good GPS system.

On Work

Most people I know work for a living. In fact some of us are working longer than we had planned since some economics have not been as certain as they once were. However, there are a few different ways in which we can think about work. Are we looking at "gainful employment," which is exchanging some of our time and energies for money? Are we looking at putting our vitality into something we love doing, which may or may not involve the exchange of money? Either way, it seems that, in order to be healthy, we'll need to be active in some pursuit, even if making money is not an issue. Seems the mind needs a focus and the body needs movement.

You'd think all of this would be self evident and hardly needs saying, but there are a number of people who tend to confuse how they attract money with what we could call right use of time and talents. When Siddhartha Gautama came forth from his meditative state and became The Buddha, he understood that we must play a part in the world. In his spiritual system, which contains ways to think and live, he included a very pragmatic path called "right work." As human beings that are spiritually based, we make an impact on life, and we can choose how this will take form in the world. One of the ways we can create a place is through work, whether money is involved or not.

In thinking through these ideas...which seem to make sense...I have to wonder...when did work get such a bad rap? When did it become a joyless chore? Could it be that much of it is done strictly for money with little regard or honor in what we do...and maybe little regard or honor for ourselves in doing it? I think that if we find ourselves in a stuck place in our work, we may find we are in a stuck place that is within ourselves, and this may cause us to be in a place that is really not for us.

The American Transcendentalist, Ralph Waldo Emerson, once wrote, "What have we to do with an evil profession?" I think that the evil consideration here does not so much have to be something illegal or destructive as much as it may mean something completely unsuitable for us. What can possibly be gained eventually if we hate what we do?

Does it take more effort to bring our best heart and mind into a circumstance than it does to just get by? No doubt, but what is the cost to us emotionally and psychologically to short ourselves in the bargain? If The Buddha's wisdom still prevails, it would be important to find the "rightness" in the use of our time and talents. I think that work done with love, creativity, integrity and real understanding cannot fail to celebrate us as we bring light right where we are. This will stand whether we are presidents of corporations, school teachers, mechanics or fence builders.

On Worship

Sometimes attending church services and the practice of worship belong together...and sometimes they don't. It is easy to be sitting in church, stomachs growling, wondering when we can go to lunch, and there is not a worshipful bone in our bodies. But then, sometimes we can be as far from a religious edifice as possible and yet be suddenly so filled with a rush of the Infinite Presence that we are driven to our knees, sometimes literally, sometimes figuratively.

Many believe that the practice of worship involves certain postures and certain physical positions. I remember putting our hands together and closing our eyes when I was a child in preparation for a prayer by the minister. I understood this as something we did when the important words, let us pray, were spoken, but I had no real idea of its relevance. Consequently I'm not sure I would consider this an act of worship. As far as I am concerned, worship involves a conscious, intentional act of connection with that which is greater than myself. Many will see this as a connection to God; others may feel it when they are close to a work of art or a spot in nature that causes an outpouring of love to spill over into our own experiences; many would not see a distinction between them.

Certainly this can happen in church. Sometimes sights, sounds, words, music and atmosphere can all swell together into a crescendo of feeling and energy that carries the participant into a larger space. The willing participant knows this as a sublime form of worship. I think that practicing Muslims have five wonderful opportunities a day to take time to worship. If one is close to the call of the *muezzin*, he or she stops activity and drops to the ground in the posture of prayer, forsaking daily demands for connection. These five times a day allow for regular, expected remembrances of the One. A skilled professor of Islamic literature once told us, his students, that even if one didn't understand the words of the Arabic call to prayer, it did not really matter. It was the *sounds of the words falling on the ear* that drew the worshipper in. There may magic in this, and certainly there is real meaning.

Of course worship can be engaged in with formality and tradition and can put the person who is really participating in a place of devotion. Rote recitations and familiar gestures can become lifeless if we're not careful, but if the opening overtures are genuine doorways to the soul that seeks, here is true wonder!

I, for one, find opportunities for worship everywhere, for the largeness of our lives is everywhere...in nature, in beautiful objects, in compelling textures, in the weaving together of words and music. Long ago when one of my grandchildren was very new and just getting used to her life in the world, I looked deep into her untroubled, infant's eyes as I held her, and for a few seconds, saw the great expanse within that gaze. I believe that together we worshipped in time and space and found the place that always awaits.

On A Safe Harbor

Who has not heard and enjoyed the stories of a safe harbor, a place where we can come in from the storm, find respite and feel secure for awhile? Probably we all have run across such tales and maybe experienced such a harbor. Do we know, however, that some harbors can be very active, heroic and life saving in themselves? There is a little known story told of boat owners who were a part of the 9/11 Boatlift the day the twin towers in New York City were attacked and brought down. Many of us do not know that hundreds of thousands of people in lower Manhattan were trapped on the island with no way to leave...except by boat. So the call went out from the Coast Guard for all boats that could do so to come to Manhattan Harbor to evacuate people who needed help. And they came...by the hundreds...Coast Guard vessels, pleasure boats, ferries, commercial boats, tug boats, big, small, constantly picking up people, taking them to safety and returning again for more. All the while no one really knew what was happening behind the billowing clouds of black smoke and ash; no one knew whether they were sailing into more attacks or not. Still they came and continued to come.

At the end of nine hours, 500,000 people had been safely transported to other harbors, a greater water rescue of people than ever done before or since, even more than at Dunkirk in WWII.

This is a magnificent story of a great city's harbor opening itself for the safety of people's leaving it for other shores, different than the harbor that welcomes those who need calm waters, but it reminds us that harbors can both receive and send forth. If we think about this a little bit, we will reflect that all harbors do not involve physical geographies; all harbors do not involve the inflow and outflow of water. Some in their ways work with the coming and going of Universal Good, and this makes it possible for human beings to realize that they are themselves natural harbors of Good. Are we not always taking in and sending out energies in life? Some people come into our lives to be sheltered for awhile; they may need our love and support as they heal or simply grow up. Then they leave; they took from us, and they gave to us, and then moved on.

I think it's good to see ourselves as safe receivers and safe senders. We may know about the giving-receiving continuum that is characteristic of life, but we may not think about how natural this continuum is within us. Left to our own devices we tend to participate in the tides that come and go in the course of our days. There is no question that we have gifts to give, even if they are as simple as the hands that hold the one who weeps or the tiny push that helps a child move off on a new bicycle. The wisdom is in knowing what is needed...the beckon or the wave.

On The Second Half of Life

Fifty years ago the second half of life for most individuals living in the western world was a fore-shortened shadow of what it was that day. Our forefathers mostly worked all their lives at one job, retired somewhere in their middle sixties and usually died within a few years, stuck with bodies not expected to last and perhaps bored to death because of blunted energies not expected to continue to be useful. That was then; this is now, and thanks to science and just plain growing older as a species, there now exists a genuine expansion of years and expectations that can include a real second life.

The probability is that we will work many jobs in the course of our lifetimes, some of the best in the second half. We have opportunities to grow far older than was once imagined and to continue to be energetic and creative for many decades because we now know that some of the best is left for the last. Some wag once said that old age is not for sissies...and with good reason. Quite naturally many people complete some of the normal accomplishments in the first half of their lives... career building, marriage and family structures, greater academic lives...and then a great vista opens before them which presents existential questions: Is this all there is? Is this all I'm good for? With the simple asking of these questions, more fun begins. Put aside the rocking chairs and hours watching television! The second half is yet to come.

I know a man who served for decades as a human resources manager of a major transit system and then crafted his love of photography into new methods of fusing pictures on wood and metal with exquisitely beautiful results. Then there is an esteemed Ivy League southern historian who shifted her energies and poured them into a whole new advanced degree in fine art. Certainly these are intelligent people, but it is not so much intellectual brilliance that causes us to open out into a second stream of expression. I think it is a sense of self development over time that one can count on. This is not the same as manufactured self esteem; this is the natural brilliance of living long enough to know that mistakes and doubts need not crush the ego, that we will survive them all and live to take another stab at doing more of what we have discovered we are capable of.

I don't think our responsibilities grow less over time. They simply change and become more universal. We may no longer have the day-to-day demands of jobs and small children, but we have more responsibilities to life itself. We who have accrued years of skills and artful living really do owe some of who we are to that which comes after us. We are not islands in a stream; we are links in a chain, and we have the love and wisdom to grace the steps of those who have not yet looked ahead to the second half of life.

On Joy

I believe that joy is an essential quality of being, and not just in human beings. I say this comfortably because it is very easy for joy to surface in the more complicated animals around us, our pets for instance. How effortless is the little I'm-so-glad-to-see-you-dance that dogs do when we come through the door? And a few cats even give us a you're-back sniff sometimes...if they're not too busy sleeping! Then again some mornings I can step out on my back deck and feel the air so sharp and crisp that it seems as if San Francisco was chiseled right out of the landscape. For no good reason at all, joy fills me, so much so that it spills over into unlooked-for tears... for no good reason at all.

I think some of this is evidence of the basic essentialness of qualities that bring meaning into life, some of which are obviously love, peace and creativity. Joy is, of course, one of these, and is different than happiness, which is usually event based. We are happy when things proceed as we would wish and unhappy when they don't, all of which suggests that our happiness is determined by things and people outside ourselves. In a way we could say that happiness is an invention, a contrivance, something we make up. Joy, on the other hand, is so naturally a part of the warp and woof of our being that we have little to do with its emergence. It can just show up at the darndest times!

In my ministerial life I have had many opportunities to officiate at funerals and memorials, no doubt some of the saddest times in peoples' lives. It has always been my commitment at these times to provide an opening for healing to occur, but, then, I cannot make this happen. There is sadness, tears, a sense of loss which is natural to our humanity, but almost without exception the remembered vitality of the one being memorialized pops into the proceedings, and smiles begin to curve upward on sad faces...and laughter visits as well. None of this trivializes the circumstance one small bit, but it simply demonstrates the undercurrent of joy that is always present and will slip through the cracks every chance it gets. Perhaps this is why so many now call end-of-life ceremonies "celebrations of life" rather than viewing them as concentrations on death.

I do not believe joy is a chemical cached in the brain, although it may be distributed chemically. Science may be able to discover it in action through neural circuits, but it does not know how to replicate it. As a believer I consider joy a quality of the

Divine...and I still don't fully understand it. In the linear folds of my thinking, it still seems a bit strange. My husband and I can be driving together for long periods of time without saying a single word...maybe not even exchanging glances, but something is taking place. How can it be that a space so silent and empty can be bursting with unstated meaning? I don't get it...and maybe I don't have to.

On Tradition

Tradition is a funny thing. For some people and entire cultures it can be the major thrust of their lives. It can be the driver of behaviors and practices from morning until night. The devout Muslim, for instance, will insert five prayer times, or salat, into his day. When it is time to pray, all activity stops, if possible, for this to take place. In Judaism certain articles of clothing have meaning; certain foods are especially prepared; certain rituals preface meals. Then again, for others there seem to be little regulating factors in their lives. Their days may move along but not seemingly according to any ritualistic procedures.

However I think that what I just said is not altogether accurate. It would seem that the thread of some kind of tradition runs through most of our lives, even very informally or unrecognized. I was made very acutely aware of this one Christmas when our extended family members were gathered...traditionally...at our home. I don't think that anyone actively thought about this until one of our granddaughters, now a mother in her own right, was overheard saying, "Well, of course we come to Nana and Grandpa's house on Christmas! It's tradition!" Who would have thought that busy kids would have honored such a memory or even cared? But then our little one now has a little one of her own and suddenly the timely, familiar gatherings all made sense. It was important to have a pond of recognition into which we could all dip our feet.

We may thumb our noses at things that appear to be out-dated, maybe even atavistic, but I think the breakdown of what has meaning happens at our peril. Certainly it is valuable to renew and re-establish ourselves on a regular basis, but when the fabric of a culture or a family is essentially torn up, I think there is a rudderlessness that converges. We don't quite know who we are or where we stand. The wonderful production of *Fiddler On The Roof* involved a family of early 20th century Russian Jews who were driven from their homes by systematic pogroms and also were bedeviled by the shifts in their own family. As we spectators watched the artful performers and heard the lush music, what we were actually viewing was the break-down of traditions. The audience's last view of the family was its emigration to the United States, and I could not help but project the future a little and wonder: Will there be a place where the family can re-establish its traditions again and find its footing?

Perhaps traditions are more important than we think, especially with the rapid, life-style changes that take place, at least in the western world. Perhaps it would be worthwhile to make sure our soul treasures are secure within ourselves, if nowhere else. And it we find ourselves at loose ends, perhaps it would be valuable to create some traditions that hold meaning for us and as gifts to those we love.

On Knowing When to Quit

To the rugged soul the word, quit, has no place. He or she will push, pull, climb over, crawl under, dig up, rebuild, restart, renew, force and cajole endlessly until everything and everyone is just plain worn out. With this much effort and energy expended, some result will usually take place, although sometimes it's questionable as to whether it was worth all the drive. But then there are the times when, no matter what, there will be nothing but "no-quit" muscles to show for what we've done, and that will have to be enough.

We may or may not be all that rugged and sometimes we will simply stop making the effort...perhaps sooner than we should...but perhaps wisely when we determine that enough really is enough. There are a lot of good reasons for knowing when to quit. Some things are simply physically impossible. Given our family genetics, no amount of prayer, exercise, good food, vitamins or steroids would generate offspring that were anywhere close to six feet tall! We could be tall minded, but the long bones in our legs were just not going to do it physically! Less obvious but just as important, there are going to be times when the heart to continue persisting just isn't there. These are usually the times when we will lacerate ourselves for not trying harder, not doing enough, even not *being* enough to finish the course, but to do this is often to overlook the fact that the motion is far more than the substance. When this discovery is eventually made and if it is hard won, it can hold both exhaustion and pain.

Divorce, for instance is one of the diciest situations when it comes to knowing when to quit. There is no question that some pairs simply don't invest enough time, love and themselves when it comes to crafting a durable relationship, and some are doomed because they don't even know how. Certainly we have known those who have had life-long marriages or partnerships, some of which were satisfying and definitely worth the effort. Others, however, became slogs, relationships with no life left, just waiting for some form of death for release.

It bears asking: When is it time to quit? When is continuance doing more harm than good? When does the comfort of enough money and stable environments gradually become sly hostage taking to keep the unsuitable in place? It is not easy to make the decision to quit a situation, and maybe it shouldn't be. Sometimes the senses of rightness and wrongness are not always present. Nice people, good people can change so much over time that the reasons for their coming together in the first place no longer exist. Nice people, good people can decide to quit, and they can do so with clear eyes, clear thinking and loving concern for themselves and one another. There is real wisdom in recognizing the time to quit before everyone is pulled to pieces with mindless effort. Each of us has start-over angels in us, and it is good to give them a place while a safe place still exists.

On Fun

Whoever decided that we get too old to be silly? Yes, there are always times when we have to straighten up and think like a mature person, but must maturity rule out just plain, old fun? Kids, especially little kids, naturally seem to know how to have fun. They have no compunctions about laughing over some little gag or making funny faces. My three-year-old great granddaughter is still at the place where I can leap out of a hiding place and say "boo", only to have her dissolve into eddies of giggles. But even kids self select around being silly. Somewhere along the way they decide they are too old to be goofy and...horrors...they quit doing so, not knowing they are heading for serious all the way, especially when sex enters the picture, and young hormones begin to flex their muscles.

I know the importance of being an informed citizen. Anyone living in a free society knows freedoms are fragile and can be snatched away through sheer inattention, let alone anything nefarious. With all the tech stuff at hand we want everything to be "transparent," which is good, I suppose, but absolutely no fun. Why do I need to know if my highly-placed government official is sleeping with another man's wife? This will catch up with him eventually. Why must I know everyone's salary? It'll probably just depress me. I could see all this gratuitous spreading of information if it actually motivated the citizenry to do something, but mostly it just gives us more to complain about. Some bloke said a long time ago that a little knowledge is a dangerous thing. What he forgot to say was that it also takes the fun out of life.

But then there was Jack...Oh, Jack was a responsible guy. He was a father and grandfather and could always be counted on to deliver anything he was in charge of, but there was always an impish sense of fun in him that lurked behind everything he did. He always had a story to tell, and we knew when he was telling "guy" stories because it was only the men who crowded around him at those times, bursting out into laughter after the stories concluded. For me it was the shaggy dog stories that were endless... "A duck went into a department store..." "How many pigmies does it take to change a light bulb?..." I felt that Jack was one of the proofs that God exists. How could it be otherwise with such an infinite supply of tales?

Suddenly one day, without asking permission from any of us, Jack took on angel wings and flew away. We were stunned. Certainly fun was still around but, without Jack, there was a big dent in it. That was a long time ago but in my mind's eye I can see him sailing into the room, smiling from ear to ear, and out it would come… "A gorilla walked into a bar…" and we'd be laughing already.

How I miss that!

30210977R00095

Made in the USA
Charleston, SC
04 June 2014